Brush, Floss, and Rinse

How to Be Healthy!

Caring for Your Teeth and Gums

by Amanda Doering Tourville   illustrated by Ronnie Rooney

PICTURE WINDOW BOOKS
Minneapolis, Minnesota

Special thanks to our advisers for their expertise:

Lauri Calanchini, RDA
CSROP Dental Careers Instructor
El Dorado, California

Terry Flaherty, Ph.D., Professor of English
Minnesota State University, Mankato

Editor: Christianne Jones
Designer: Tracy Davies
Page Production: Michelle Biedscheid
Art Director: Nathan Gassman
The illustrations in this book were created with
ink and watercolor.

Picture Window Books
151 Good Counsel Drive
P.O. Box 669
Mankato, MN 56002-0669
877-845-8392
www.picturewindowbooks.com

Printed in the United States of America.

 All books published by Picture Window Books
are manufactured with paper containing at least
10 percent post-consumer waste.

Library of Congress Cataloging-in-Publication Data
Tourville, Amanda Doering, 1980-
Brush, floss, and rinse : caring for your teeth and
gums / by Amanda Doering Tourville ; illustrated
by Ronnie Rooney.
p. cm. — (How to be healthy!)
Includes index.
ISBN-13: 978-1-4048-4805-4 (library binding)
1. Teeth—Care and hygiene—Juvenile literature. 2. Dental
care—Juvenile literature. I. Rooney, Ronnie. II. Title.
RK63.T68 2009
617.6′01—dc22   2008006422

You need your teeth to chew your food. You need your teeth to talk and smile. It's important to take care of your teeth and gums. There are many ways to keep them clean and healthy.

Kyle and Alan brush their teeth every night before bed. They brush the top, front, and back of each tooth.

A sticky layer forms on your teeth. This layer is called plaque. Brushing helps remove the plaque from your teeth.

5

After brushing, Kyle and Alan ask their mom to help them floss.

Their mom helps them move the floss between their teeth.

Flossing helps remove food and plaque that gets stuck between your teeth. It keeps your teeth and gums healthy.

7

Alan and Kyle do not chew the ice in their water glasses.

Never chew on hard objects like candy or ice. They can chip or break your teeth.

They know that chewing on hard objects
can damage their teeth.

Alan and Kyle brush their teeth every morning. They brush for two minutes to make sure their teeth are clean.

Use only a small amount of toothpaste. It should be no bigger than a pea. Do not swallow the toothpaste.

Alan plays hockey after school. He wears a plastic mouth guard to protect his teeth.

When playing a contact sport, it's important to protect your teeth.

Alan and Kyle choose apples instead of cookies for a snack. They know that sugar is bad for their teeth.

Eating sugary snacks can cause your teeth to decay, which can cause cavities.

Alan pours glasses of milk for himself and Kyle. Milk will keep their teeth strong.

Milk contains calcium. Calcium helps you grow strong bones and teeth.

Kyle and Alan use fluoride rinse after brushing and flossing. They swish it around for one minute.

Fluoride keeps your teeth from decaying. Children must be at least 6 years old to use fluoride safely.

Alan and Kyle go to the dentist for checkups.

They listen when the dentist tells them how to keep their teeth and gums clean and healthy.

Everyone should have his or her teeth cleaned and checked once or twice a year.

To Learn More

More Books to Read

Bagley, Katie. *Brush Well: A Look at Dental Care.*
    Mankato, Minn.: Bridgestone Books, 2002.
Keller, Laurie. *Open Wide: Tooth School Inside.*
    New York: Henry Holt, 2000.
Radabaugh, Melinda Beth. *Going to the Dentist.*
    Chicago: Heinemann Library, 2004.

On the Web

FactHound offers a safe, fun way to find Web sites related to topics in this book. All of the sites on FactHound have been researched by our staff.

1. Visit *www.facthound.com*
2. Type in this special code: 1404848053
3. Click on the FETCH IT button.

Your trusty FactHound will fetch the best sites for you!

Look for all of the books in the How to Be Healthy! series:

Brush, Floss, and Rinse: Caring for Your Teeth and Gums
Fuel the Body: Eating Well
Get Up and Go: Being Active
Go Wash Up: Keeping Clean

Index